SELECTED LAGHUKATHAS OF SANTOSH SUPEKAR

TRANSLATION BY: KALPANA BHATT (BHOPAL)

SANTOSH SUPEKAR | TRANSLATION BY: KALPANA BHATT

Contents

Contents

Contents

Few Lines From Writer's Pen

Translation of literature is a very complicated work .Translator must be careful about the essence of the creation.His main goal is to deliver the original meaning (not word)and make the final result to read.That 's why he always avoids word to word translation of any composition.

It is the matter of pride for me that Honourable Kalpna Bhattji selected my some significant Laghukthas for this vital collection.By doing this work she is not only creating history but also expanding the range of Hindi Laghukatha and Literature.

I am very much influenced from the studiousness and assidousness of both, Honourable Kalpna Bhatt ji and Honourable Chandresh kumar Chhatlaniji for their tireless hard work.

Thanks a lot again to both litterateurs.

Waiting for your response.

Santosh Supekar

31,Sudama Nagar ,

Ujjain {M.P..}

9424816096

The Story Behind This Book

It so happened that Mr.Santosh Supekar ji had sent me 4 of his Laghukatha Sangrah. It was in 2020 before lockdown.
When I went through his laghukathas I heard a sound from within me saying, "Why don't you try to translate these laghukathas? This would give you an opportunity to do some creativity."
I was a bit confused as I was not sure that Supekar ji would allow me to proceed. But then it so happened that randomly 5 of his laghukathas were translated by me and I sent them to him. He was very glad, and his motivational words inspired me and gave me confidence. He got all of the 5 laghukathas published. The chapter was closed.
Meanwhile I got a job work of translating some laghukathas and short-stories from a publisher . I was trying to complete them, meanwhile once again Supekar ji's sangrah were calling me.
So along with the job-work, whenever I got some time his laghukathas called me for getting them translated from hindi to english.
It was a different experience, but was once again confused as to whether I should continue or should talk to Supekar ji. So one day I put him a message that I wish to translate some more of his laghukathas and told him that I wish them to be published as an E-book.
He was not only glad but he also gave me permission to proceed and Lo! It was done..
Once again I went through his books one by one and once again a question aroused in my mind as to how many laghukatha's from each book should be taken?
But then from one book I selected the ones which I liked and marked them. Later on when I counted they were 14 in number and now it became easy for me and then 14 laghukatha's from each sangrah were decided.
When Supekar ji asked me from where will you get them published

? One name clicked to me and that was of Dr.Chandresh Chhatlani. Both of us talked to him regarding this project and I was glad that he agreed upon to get it published as myself and Supekar ji both of us are fully unaware of making an e-book.

This is how with the kind support of both of my seniors this project could be accomplished and now it is in your hands.

My wish was and is to try to reach youth so that they can read laghukathas in a language they can read and understand. The world is becoming digital and the youth are reading on different digital platforms.

I hope that readers would go through these and would frankly give their reviews .

But before I end up to this article I would like to thank Respected Supekar ji who not only gave me permission to proceed but also guided me whenever I needed and so was Mr. Chhatlani ji. I thank both of them for their kind motivation, support and co-operation to have this project accomplished.without which I couldn't have been able to complete it.

I dedicate this book to my baba, Dr.Satishraj Pushkarna ji who was my soul father who taught me the meaning of laghukatha and it's technical aspects along with him I can't forget Mr.Ravi Prabhakar, a very loveable person and a brother to me have had met on social media. He used to tell me, "Di I wish you to do your work with dedication and I wish my di to be seen every where on the platform of laghukatha."

I cannot forget them for all their love, affection and their guidance. Both of them passed away in the year 2021, this was a great personal loss for me..But you shall always remain with me in whatever I write . I also am thankful to Shri. Yograj Prabhakar Sir, Editor of half yearly magazine namely 'Laghukatha Kalash' fully dedicated to Laghukatha. He is a real friend, philosopher and a guide for me who has always motivated me and guided me whenever I have asked for.

Thank you all for being a part of life.

And now in the last but not the least I shall wait for your response.

Thanking you

- **Kalpana Bhatt**

Bhopal

Best Wishes

At the outset, I would like to quote Charles W. Eliot, who once said, "Books are the quietest and most constant of friends; they are the most accessible and wisest of counsellors, and the most patient of teachers."

I also understand that the biggest mystery in our Human life is not our intelligence, but our creativity, which is sometimes beyond intelligence.

Books are the written format of this mystery. Books guide us to lead the future and to understand the past.

Laghuaktha is the mode of literature which has the completeness of a single spot of everything which may be thought of. In a Laghukatha, sometimes you may listen to the music of a drop of rain and sometimes whole rain in a single sound of music.

Shri Santosh Supekar and Kalapna Bhatt ji both are renowned writers of Laghukatha, therefore, undoubtedly, it can be said that, this collection of the translated literary work of Shri Supekar by Smt. Bhatt includes all the parameters of Laghukatha and would be useful for the society and the individual person.

My best wishes.

- Dr. Chandresh Kumar Chhatlani

3 PA 46, Prabhat Nagar, Sector-5, Hiran Magari, UDAIPUR - 313 002 (Rajasthan)

9928544749, chandresh.chhatlani@gmail.com

CHAPTER ONE

Weak Nerve

Unfortunately, a piece of diamond, was lying near a stone on an unclaimed land. No one had yet recognized and picked it up. One day irritatingly he with an attitude proclaimed to the stone, "I know the status of a human being. Whenever a person would recognize me, he would keep me with great love, and no one will ever bother to even look at you."

"You may be well versed with their status" The stone answered, " I know their weak nerve. You will be kept in their safety vault but if anyone paints me with any particular colour, then undoubtedly the same people would pour aromatic flowers on me, would lit incense sticks in front of me, would bow to me. Not only this, if any one would dare insult me then they would not even hesitate in shedding blood."

CHAPTER TWO

Culture Express

Thomas sahib is from Kerela, Harmindersingh is from Punjab, I am from Maharashtra, Rambabu singh is from Bihar, Arif Khan is from Rajasthan. We are all good friends, even our families are very closely connected, so only we do celebrate Christmas, Onam, Baisakhi, Mahalakshmi Pooja, Chhath Pooja, Eid and all other festivals are very well known to us and we celebrate all of them with joy and delight. The reason! We all serve with Railways, all together, in the same department, since years.

The Indian Railways, you see does not only join cities, rather it acts a common juncture for various cultures.

CHAPTER THREE

Politics and Political Science

Today in the city his party's general meeting is to be conducted, in which they were going to thank him. Huge hoardings were hanged-up at many places , in which the word best-wishes was present everywhere. The newspapers are all full with his posters.

Sometimes back... he and I were colleagues while studying. I was an average student, but today I am just pulling up myself while working in a private firm. He was not able to study properly in the Mahavidhyalaya, but today he has reached at a better place.

Why did he have to leave his studies?...Oh yes, I recollect, he had failed in Political Science...

Later on he started participating in politics and there he would always succeed. Not only in securing good marks, but also getting more votes.

CHAPTER FOUR

Presence of Happiness

"Arey, where were you for two days?" Rameshji asked Abrahim Sahib as soon as he saw him in the office, " didn't see me, was there any urgency?"

"Yes friend, I was on leave and had gone in a marriage procession.

" A marriage procession! Whose?"

" A family has come to live in my neighborhood since a month."

" Has the relationship turned to be so strong in just about a month that you had to take a leave?"

"A strong relationship is not an issue at all." Abrahim Sahib's tone was serious, "actually they are very poor, and have no any such known people and relatives in this city. The son too is a very simple and straight-forward boy. He had no friend of him, so when they asked me to join them, looking into their status and requirement I could not deny. I don't repent in taking leave from the office and joining them in their happy moments.

CHAPTER FIVE

Condemnation

In the twilight, near the big four-square there was a park wherein two drunkards with all belongings were alert to find a safer place. Looking around on all the four sides they saw that at one corner some children were making noise while playing cricket, on the other side some retired old people were busy gossiping, on the third side ground-nut vendors were seated calculating their income. "That corner would be perfect." One of the drunkard said.

"Yes of-course! Now let us come daily and sit in that corner, it is the most safest place as it well covered."

And in a couple of minutes, a foul smell of opium and the hemp plant (Gaanjaa) spread all over.

That covered place was as such a neglected place, only 0.001 percent people would visit this place once in a blue moon.

That 'covered place' name was- A Martyr's Statue.

CHAPTER SIX

A Boisterous Laugh

An oath taking ceremony was going on- In the name of God that I shall always work with integrity.

"Ha ha ha" , a man from amongst the crowd gave a loud Horse-laugh.

"Who are you?" surprisingly I asked him, "and why are you laughing?"

"I try to be present everywhere, wherever an oath is being taken in the name of truth, either it is an oath taking ceremony of politicians, or an oath taken by keeping hands on holy books like Geeta/Quraan, or Hippocratic oath in the medical field...

"Ok, ok what then who are you?"

"You couldn't yet recognize me? " again with a loud boisterous laugh he said, " I am a Lie ! I feel more happier when my strongest enemy ' The Truth' is being insulted the most only at such occasions.

CHAPTER SEVEN

Strange, But The Truth

Among the interesting Questioner a question was put up

"How can one know about the Civility and Culture of the modern People?"

Lot many answers came up, some came up with the spoken language, some said about their living behavior, then some believed that their kinsfolk could be used as the measuring device for their Civility and Culture. But the exact and appropriate answer was-

If one wishes to know about a particular man's civility and culture then one needs to fumble in with the thrown out garbage, the eating habits of the related person in particular, civility, culture all would be found out from that garbage.

CHAPTER EIGHT

An Emotional Stroke

"Papa, Papa" a boy studying in an English medium school and a son of a Hindi Lecturer asked, " what does the number fifty and ten mean?"

"Oh my dear son! Don't you know the meaning of the number fifty and ten? Sixty."

"Oh, Thank You Papa."

Just then he recollected that our Independence too was sixty years old, while listening to the patriotic songs played then.

"The number fifty and ten means sixty."

"Sixty or the number fifty and ten?"

He was giving a thought.

CHAPTER NINE

The Truth of Teacher's Day

After 35 years of his dedicated services he was given a grand informal Thanks giving party on Teacher's Day. He was happily returning homewards , suddenly from some house he heard a call from someone, "Sir, Sir."

"Arey Jagannath" He had not forgotten a twenty years old brilliant student, " Do you live here?"

"Congratulations Sir." While touching his feet Jagannath said, " Please be seated Sir, Let me ask someone to prepare tea for you." Both of them went inside, there they saw a young boy who was behaving in a very abnormal way.

"Jagannath, is he your son? What is wrong with him?" He asked Jagannath as soon as he entered the room.

"What should I tell you Sir?" With wet eyes Jagannath said, " He had been a brilliant child since his childhood. He scored first class even in his Second Year, then God only knows what happened that he failed in his Third Year. He told us that he had done well in his exams but after his results he was shocked. It has been three years now, he has been living like a corpse , my poor only son. Just leave it Sir, Please have your tea."

The sweet tea and the recently achieved award now seemed to bitter and sallow... Looking at the verdict of the politics spread all over in modern Education.

CHAPTER TEN

Future

He was driving his new car in a city having narrow lanes and dense market and by stopping each and every passer-by was asking the same question,

" Is there any closed shop here?"

His wife got irritated and could not stop herself, "What a inane question you are asking? Have we come here for marketing or to visit a closed shop?"

"My dear wife, this is not a inane question, this is a question in future." He said calmly, "I am looking for a closed shop so that I can park our car there. In future we would have so many cars that every car driver will ask the same question in the market."

CHAPTER ELEVEN

Kitchen

A couple had come to see their huge but vacant land and was discussing a plan for their future bungalow. But suddenly they had a dispute while discussing about as to what should be the exact location of their kitchen? The dispute grew to such an extent that both of them sat in their own car and drew back.

A laborer couple who was then looking at this couple with fun was cooking their food on a temporary stove made out of four to five bricks and was enjoying their food.

CHAPTER TWELVE

The Only Son

"I am going to retire after two weeks" Devisinghji said this to his sub-ordinate Francis, "I shall get Rupees Twenty five lacs only on my retirement. I am not able to decide as to which of my son I should give this amount."

"How many sons do you have?"

"Three."

"No, at present you have only one son."

"Why did you say no? What exactly do you mean by this?" Devisingh ji said this in the state of provocation.

"I mean to say that at present you have only one son and that is your retirement amount. Remember my words that till the amount remains with you, all your three sons of yours will be with you. After all you are very smart enough." Francis said this very calmly.

CHAPTER THIRTEEN

Devil's Followers

Two religious gurus were discussing-

"I have always taught my followers to live in peace and to respect all religions."

"I too have taught the same thing there is no happiness than living in peace."

Just then their followers had a big fight on the earth people were killing each other and there was bloodshed all over.

"These are not my followers." One of the two gurus said this in astonishment. The other too said the same in astonishment and in a repulsive manner.

"Then whose followers are these followers?"

"Mine" A Devil who was sitting near them sarcastically said this, "On Earth; most of the followers are mine. The religious places may belong to you, but the people going there are all in my control."

CHAPTER FOURTEEN

The Great Food-Producer

"Papa" a six year old child asked his father while opening his copy, "How is Roti made? Tell me what to write?"

"Oh how silly? Very easy, it is made with flour, write it down." His father hastily said this while putting on his shoes.

"No beta" the old grandfather who was a former farmer, said this in a serious tone, "Roti is made from wheat flour and wheat is grown in fields. It is a farmer who works hard in extreme heat and gets wet in the rains while farming. Monsoon plays hide-n-seek. Farmer has to shed lots of sweat, and this is how a roti is made." The grandfather was telling this while he was recollecting his past.

CHAPTER FIFTEEN

A Frightening Anxiety

A few days before on T.V., I had watched a dreadful scenario of agitated borders in which lot many killings and blood-shed had occurred, which not only did I remember but also it gave birth to a fretful shivering...

In this scenario a pitiful-very pitiful father of a country indulged in war, terrorism, a country facing refugee problems leaves his small child in other country's border through a broken fence of his own border. While doing this he could not stop his tears rushing out. The little boy who was forced to leave his father, his facial expressions were such that any cruel to cruelest person too would not have stopped crying...

It seemed that someone was just pushing his beloved son into a flooded ocean, from the shore, beyond any expectation, in an expectation that he may survive in the other land, as it was most possible that he may for sure die in this land where there was so much of violence, killing and blood-shed.

Such an uproar and agitation exists in many of such borders. Born from the piercing and heartbreaking screaming of mankind does exists in my frightening thoughts, the scenario turning into general ...

CHAPTER SIXTEEN

Mark of Identification

It was night. In winter season, while climbing on the lonely long, high stairs of a bridge, now I was repenting. I had with me Government's sixty thousand rupees in my bag. Being late in the office and with an intension to reach home early, I could not avoid my temptation to choose this shortcut. In this chilly winter also salt water droplets were falling from my face, it was difficult to judge whether this was because of fast climbing or my fear. I felt to throw away my coat even. Just then my pace and my heartbeat increased when from a distance and in the midst I saw that a long man wearing an overcoat was coming behind. "Oh my God, I am dead... he must be some marauder, he must have judged that I have cash with me, what shall I do? My God..." My paces as well as my fear were increasing, and I was sweating too. "The bridge too is so long. In this desolated road he may very easily rob me. It is fine if he robs me, it is Government's money, I shall launch a F.I.R. or will repay recovery...but what if he pierces a knife and takes out my intestines...Yes this too is possible, it would be easy to take away the bag from near my dead body, now it is all on God's mercy... Pushpa will get the job after me, but kids... I was overwhelmed with sadness, "My kids are too small, what will happen to them..." The possibilities of the unforeseen had taken me to a great extent.

Till now I could not hear his footsteps near me, I tried to come over my fear and turned behind... "Oh, what is in his hands? O.....h..." I was bit relaxed, "How come I did not pay attention towards this." Now I had regained my senses suddenly, I felt assured. The fast pumping heart was now pumping normal, “This cannot be of any robber or a marauder, it symbolizes a hard-working person, tiffin.

Still he was behind me but he had gone far beyond from my reflection.

CHAPTER SEVENTEEN

Last Wish

"What was your last wish while you were dying?" A soul asked another.

"One only", he moaned while giving a reply, "I was anyhow able to manage cash for my son's admission in medical." The moaning had now turned into grief, "How I had a wish to see his Degree, his clinic but due to cancer nothing of the sort could happen."

"Oh!"

"Tell me about yourself" Coming out of his memories he asked the other soul, "What was your last wish, while dying?"

"Mine... ha-ha-ha-ha" the first soul irritatingly laughed, "There is no any comparison of any sort with you, even you will laugh hearing it... My last wish was that someone would cover me up with a blanket, a thick-soft, but a woolen blanket... I had died because of cold on an open street...

CHAPTER EIGHTEEN

Guinea Pigs

I started looking for a seat as soon as I entered the train, though it was crowded I could get a seat near the cabin's corner. As the train moved on cool breeze blew in, I was a bit relaxed and so I turned my eyesight on all directions, some villagers were seated in front of me. "Where do you want to go?" Just to kill time I asked, "Jaipur, Sahib, that I shall be getting a sum of one thousand rupees as a daily wage therein." He was much excited while saying this.

"Rupees one thousand only per-day! Which company is offering this?" I was now alert I tried to concentrate on him.

"No Sahib, It is not a company, some Hos...hos hospital sort of place, Manku from our village had told us, he had said that they give some tablet before work, that gives us strength to work."

"A tablet? They make people work after giving tablet? What sort of work is this? What has your Manku said...?" I was doubtful.

"No Sahib, We don't know about his whereabouts since some time."

"Giving tablets, a place somewhat like hospital? One thousand rupees per day, will be paid to them?" These questions were really bothering me. I was much terrified, "Is that it?" Recently heard incidence was clicking over my mind, "is it possible that these poor villagers used as guinea pigs? Guinea pig: those rats, pigs on whom medicines are examined. So these people are going to be used as rats? How should I convince them that... but this poor people are in greed of One thousand Rupees." While I was thinking, instead of those villagers I could see rats, giving a laughter,scrubbing tobacco, in lack of knowledge or in greed they are getting into death's cage, those poor rats, guinea pigs...

CHAPTER NINETEEN

Between the Whirlpool

As soon as Rampaal returned back home from field, Reema who was teaching her son got up and went into their kitchen.

"Mummy, Atleast help me to complete my homework." Tinku shouted extremely loudly.

"Beta, Ask your Baba to help you out. Let me heat up the food."

"Baba, Baba, kindly tell me a sentence using cloud as a word."

"What? Did you say cloud?" Tiresome and irritated Rajpaal was going to scold the kid but he stopped as soon as he heard the word 'cloud'.

Looking at the clouds in the month of March he was already tensed, "Write it down beta, Clouds are very important for farmers. It creates problems in case when it doesn't rain on time and it creates even more problems when it rains before time.

CHAPTER TWENTY

Regretful Past

"What Papa?" hesitatingly Vivek asked, "Are you calling from Bus-stand? But you were supposed to come by train, isn't it?"

"The train is late, we shall talk later on." Parmanandji in a stunned voice said, "come immediately to the bus-stand and pick us up, We are waiting for you near A.T.M."

Vivek in a panic reached bus-stand then Paramanandji narrated him the whole incidence, "Beta, we were all asleep in our coach, just then there was a chaos at Bina station, many youngsters, who had to appear some exam for some job, forcibly climbed upon in our coach, they woke up all those who were sleeping, started quarreling and took up to fighting. They started molesting ladies and young girls. We were much scared, your sister was then in a washroom. Something clicked us and we called her up and asked her to get down from train from there only, and both of us made an attempt to come out, reach bus-stand and after catching a bus arrived here, but do not know..." Parmanandji was severely shivering, "What would have occurred with the rest of those poor passengers?"

"O....h" hearing to the incidence he exclaimed with this as if gas had been released from a balloon and he was stuck into an incidence occurred four years back in his past, when he too with some of jobless youngsters in a team had climbed upon a train in the similar way and had created a havoc thus harassing and threatening passengers. He had succeeded in saving himself then but today he found himself in the dock.

CHAPTER TWENTY-ONE

Those 'Prefixes' and ' Suffixes'

A debate was going-on on television, a leader's son was charged for committing a rape. In a victorious tone the leader was conveying, "My son is innocent, someone is trying to trap him in such a case, in order to lower down our prestige. He does not even know that girl and I demand for an investigation, after all oil and truth must come out.

On the other hand the relatives of the victim with a heavy heart and weeping were accusing him with one after another charge, and were demanding for a capital punishment. Leaders from other parties too were supporting them. This too was shown that one of the victim's relative was declaring the leader's son to be non-guilty...

"God knows what the truth was!" Amongst the people sitting in front of television and the ones seating in the studio, some were repeatedly saying, "God knows what the truth was..."

Just then from some corner a sobbing sound could be heard. "Who is it?" I cautiously asked, "Who is in there?"

"It is me my dear brother." He sobbingly answered, "I am the truth! As such all my tears are dried up after having had cried for so many times, since last so many decades, but now I am crying because instead of a complete sentence, people now utter only one single word for me and these days I find no any difference between a sentence formation and a word formation.

"What do you mean?"

"I mean to say that when all say, "don't know, what the truth is' then my identity is hurt, making me more suspicious, these sentences do not seem to be a sentence, rather it seems to be a word and these fools, add either 'prefix' or 'suffix' on the either sides of these words , 'don't know' and 'what is it!"

CHAPTER TWENTY-TWO

Sunlight All over

“What have you done? Just wait, I was out for two days, you have completely destroyed the structure of this chaukhandi (a sitting room which was usually located in the centre of the house, above which large sized ventilation was constructed so as to get sunlight throughout the house). Ramakantji scolded the laborers working in their under-constructive house, “Listen, the above ventilation has to made more bigger, so that sunlight can enter properly, but you people won’t understand, “Wouldn’t you?” looking at his anger, his wife and children went away then he once again looked at the faces of the laborers, “Am I not right? The sunlight is so important in every house, we get vitamin D through it, which strengthens our body and bones, you all are laborers, you must have made a centralized place at your homes too to get sunlight, isn’t it?”

“W...? sunlight ?” Listening to his question and wiping his sweat a young labor laughed, “Babuji, Where do we have our homes? We live on pavement. There we have sunlight all over, from morning till evening.”

CHAPTER TWENTY-THREE

A Hole in the System

"Hey... What is this?" Nilesh put a heavy break while driving a bike and disgustingly he put his hand on the nose because of foul smell, How is it that in the middle of the road there is line of the garbage and the line is going far more ahead...in this tenure of cleanliness how come...?

"Brother" a cart-man who had heard his murmuring said, " A garbage van has recently passed, collecting all the wastage and garbage ! The lower portion of the container may have had some holes, so only when the garbage van is running ahead and the garbage is dropping out...

CHAPTER TWENTY-FOUR

A Mystery

"How hot it is? Absolutely harsh! Burning and life threatening" family members were talking, "There is no any sign of rain, not even this time."

"Yes... It is very difficult to survive in this humid and dryness." Looking at the ceiling fan Minni said, "The fan may run at higher speed, things don't change, the mood gets off because of this heat...but have you noticed one thing, Raju, "Have you watched Papa? He has never complained of feeling hot even in this worst temperature, rather he seems to be much happier, doesn't he?

"Yes, of course, you are absolutely correct." Raju positively nodded his head and said, "You have pointed out a perfect point Minnu. Papa, tell us, what exactly is the mystery behind this."

"Yes Papa, Please tell us today..."

"My children, I too feel the heat, after all I too am a human being, but during these hot summers the bigger dam nearby partially gets dried up." While saying this Ramnathji's eyes were glowing, "and through it our village is clearly visible. After the dam was constructed it came to be considered as a flooding area. My village, my birthplace and even my work-place where I have had been working for thirty-eight years. This is the only season when I can see it and this is the mystery behind by happiness." Thinking about the scenario of the dried dam made his eyes we

CHAPTER TWENTY-FIVE

What is that?

"You can order for one thousand bricks if they are so required. Do you get me?"

"Mummy, what is a brick?" Listening to Saurabh talking to the labor contractor of their under-construction house, his four year son asked him.

"Beta, do you see these red-red rectangular shaped stone like... these are bricks."

"What work does she do?"

"Beta, these do not work, rather they are used in some work, they are used to construct walls, houses."

"And"

"And what that is all..."

"Then mummy, what is that?" The son pointed out his fingers in other directions where by a labor was sleeping on a pillow of four bricks, and a woman labor lighting a temporary stove made up of six to eight bricks. Even these are bricks. Aren't they?"

CHAPTER TWENTY-SIX

Newborn Fright

"Shall we go to Nareshji? He lives nearby doesn't he?" Namita tried to make Sumeet recollect.

"No"

"Why" looking at Sumeet's facial expression Namita was now furious, "Have you had a quarrel with him? You used to visit him very often in past. Why have you broken this chain now?"

"......"

"Turn the car, let us visit them for ten minutes, maintaining a relationship is both sided , if we do not visit them then..."

"I have said no, we shan't visit."

"What no-no? After all I should know the reason behind it."

"Reason" stopping the car on a side Sumeet said, "As such nothing has happened. You know it very well that his nine year old son calls me 'a bad uncle, because of him the children living nearby too have started saying the same, may be because of my dark complexion and the small-pox's scars they too have started. Until now I did not feel anything considering them as children but now the case is different." Hearing mob's noise from outside, he raised up the glasses of their car and continued, "In the present times it takes no time to create a fuss and mob lynching, if any crazy person hears to the kid's words and come to some absurd conclusions and gather a crowd than... in such a case what would be the condition of an innocent person, you can very well understand this, it is for this particular reason that I have been trying to avoid visiting there...

"Oh, so this is the case, now that what and how the kids and his family members to be convinced? They will not agree to this." The mob's noise was becoming violent, hearing this Namita was in fright and she said, "But I shall agree unto you. Let us all go home."

CHAPTER TWENTY-SEVEN

Uncovered Truth

"It is now twenty years tenure of my job." I said this while drinking sweet tea but with a bitter mouth, "But, I have never come across such an arrogant boss."

"Huh, you are right." Gulping away the left over tea Ashok agreed upon my view-point, "He is not only arrogant but also a person of low standard, I have never come across such a cheap type of person, I too have completed nineteen years job tenure but this type of bad period has never come before."

"But my job tenure has is for twenty two years!" A youth in shabby clothes and of about twenty five years old, who was seated next to them, exclaimed this while drinking tea.

"Twenty two years? Looking down upon him and sarcastically I asked him, "How come twenty years of job tenure? As to how old are you?"

"I have been picking and collecting garbage since I was four, then I was not even able to walk properly" it seemed that he sighed while uttering the new fact, "At present I am twenty six, now tell me haven't I completed a tenure of twenty two years of my job?"

CHAPTER TWENTY-EIGHT

Serious Laughter

"Hey Chhotu, listen" I called upon the boy of about twelve-thirteen years who was washing dishes in a tea-making cupola and ordered, "Go and get me some sugar along with a spoon."

"He..he..he" the boy gave a laughter and brought back the two things.

"What are you laughing for?" I asked him angrily, "Have I made a mistake? Or is it because I summoned you as Chhotu?"

"Yes Saabji, actually all customers summon me with the same name, not only me but also the boy similar to my age; working in the cupola just in the opposite side pointing towards that boy he said, "people call that Bunty too with the same name inspite of the fact that both of us are the eldest of all other family members, we are not small and the house cores are on our shoulders and we run our houses.

The boy who was laughing till now turned serious.

CHAPTER TWENTY-NINE

An Application

Like each year Raghvendra along with his wife and children had come to his parental town-ship this year also. As he could not get leaves from his job, did not allow him to stay here for more than a week or so. How much did he wish that his parents should come and stay with him at Ahmadabad for a year or at-least for two-three months He and his wife Anita wished that their kids get to grow in Joint family so also lot of love from their grand-parents . For the same purpose they had constructed a flat with five rooms but, for some unknown reason his parents used to come occasionally. May be once in a year that to, for a couple of days.

"Babuji, you and ma11a should visit here not for 4-6 days but for four to six months. It is very hurtful when you go away so soon." Last time when he had said this to his father, he had said, "beta, I have many a times said this to you that that small town-ship is our birthplace as well as our work-place. We don't find ourselves at ease except there. Yours flat in this city though it is big enough we can't stay here for more days."

Today in the evening he entered into his room. He switched on the light and went near a box kept in a corner. His childhood's the most favorite wooden box. Whenever did he come here, he would open this box at least for once. In general eagerness he opened it. Class sixth-seventh-eighth course books, his old times books, geometry box, football shoes with nails in the foot-heels, an extra dress for N.C.C. , old photo-album and what not ! His wish to look at them never was less even though he looked at them again and again. Suddenly he caught a sight with a polythene bag. He opened it. He saw small pieces of paper cuttings which had turned yellow now. He started reading the matter written on them one by one-babuji...babuji...babuji ! These were the collection of the cuttings in which he used to write his demands. While reading them he could not stop his tears. He was his babuji's lovable Raghvendra, Raghav. Whatever he wanted something, he could not ask his babuji so he would write in on a paper cutting and would put it in his father's pocket. And it never did happen when his babuji would forget to bring his things or fulfill his wishes... Raghvendra who was till now lost in his thoughts with wet eyes, suddenly was dazzled. He put all the paper-cuttings back into the polythene-bag and put them all back in the box. Instantaneously he made a paper-cutting and wrote on it- babuji, I very sincerely wish that you and amma come and stay with us in Ahmadabad for two-three months every year. I assure that you will not feel uncomfortable.

Yours Raghav.

He put it into his pocket of babuji's kurtaa and his hands were trembling in excitement par he was fully assured that his application would not be rejected.

CHAPTER THIRTY

Screams of laughter

'A never ending war has begun in Iraq' reading these news the common men at first gave a smile then their smile turned into explosion of laughter.

The laughter was echoing in the entire room and in his thoughts he could hear echo sounds of too many hurdles of his life similar to the cannon shooting sound- his father who was suffering from cancer was to be taken to Mumbai but, the reservation was not yet done...

He had purchased an auto-rickshaw for his young son but because he could not run it for even a single day, the installment of the loan was yet to be paid...

His daughter's marriage has broken; he is being forced to look like a happy man in front of the society by neglecting all those who are pointing fingers, he has to show himself as a happy person so as to re-settle his daughter...

One of the walls of his kitchen had become hollow, the toilet was jammed, and current was passing through in the geyser, all these things needed to be repaired, he could not have had enough money nor was able to arrange any, P.F balance too was not left much...

'Huh' a never ending war going on in Iraq! He murmured, "A common man fights a dangerous war daily! He fights, he is defeated and again he stands up and fights once again." He once again laughed and laughed and laughed. He himself couldn't realize whether it was his laughter or he was screaming.

CHAPTER THIRTY-ONE

Into a disguised form

On a river bank an old man was in search of something.

"Whom are you searching?" lawlessness asked him.

"Me..." with a slight hesitation the old man said, "I am searching the bank whereby lions and goats together used to drink water."

"Ha...ha...ha..."lawlessness gave an exploited laughter and said, "May be in the near past such a bank did exist, but these days you will find many, whereby lions and goats drink water from the same bank."

"Is it? Tell me where?" The old man's eyes were widened in surprise.

"Don't search them here, as elections are to be conducted. Rather you should be at the doors of the residents in the early morning. There you will find too many banks and lot many lions and goats, all in their disguised forms.

CHAPTER THIRTY-TWO

Pricking Factum

As soon as Ashok ji saw Vibhaji bringing water in the drawing-room he complained to her saying, “Why didn’t you attend Bunty’s birthday party day-before-yesterday?”

“Oh yes bhaisahab” Vibhaji’s seemed to be bit hesitant, “How I wished to attend it but was helpless as Pinky’s exams are going on.”

Ashok ji had to make some other complaints also he said, “Also, you didn’t come to my new house’s opening last year!”

“Yes you are correct.” She felt more hesitant than before, “Then too I had wanted to come but Babloo’s exams were going on during that period.”

“Oh, but do come whenever you can!” Ashok ji ended his complaints by saying this but the fact was still pricking him that the exams so conducted are not only for kids but along with it, it takes sacrifices of each and every homemaker, every year and years ahead, her relationships, her freedom, her wishes.

CHAPTER THIRTY-THREE

(On the) corpse of Sympathy

He was passing by through the main ground of the city where he could hear lots of noise. When he reached near then he saw that a stage was built up on that ground and thousands of people were quarrelling below the stage. They were pushing each other, tearing each other's clothes."

"Hey...y...y..."he stopped one of those men and asked, "What is this going on? Why are you all fighting with each other?"

"From which world are you from?" that man stared at him from top to bottom and said; "Look there, just in your front' pointing out towards a tree, "In front of the whole assembly a poor man committed a suicide."

"Oh!" seeing the corpse hanging on the tree he was stunned. Just then he seemed to recollect something so asked, "Why couldn't anyone try to stop him while he was trying to commit a suicide."

"Hey my dear brother for the same reason these people are fighting. Each one is them is blaming others that why didn't he stop him?' And then he once again joined the men quarreling and got occupied in the quarrel.

CHAPTER THIRTY-FOUR

One's Helplessness

A doctor habituated to increase his fees often when on that day did not charge the increased fees from the last patient; after he was gone the doctor's wife asked him, "You charged all of your patients with the increased fees then why did you not do the same with that fellow, is he known to you?"

"No! not at all. If at all did I know him than you must have known him too." The doctor said, " but somehow I felt that this patient may not be able to pay it."

"How did you feel this? According to me his condition seemed to quite good enough' his wife said as if recollecting something, "He was in decent clothes."

"It is not clothes, but his chapels, you should have seen his chapels." The doctor was trying to bring out the reality, "That self-respected person may seem to be in decent dress, but he was wearing two different chapels, different chapels from different pairs."

CHAPTER THIRTY-FIVE

The Name of the Movie

"Isn't it the same mall which was in news recently in almost every newspaper?" Looking at a five storied building he could recollect something, that it was an illegal constructed mall," He then saw that the mall's building was a beautiful piece of modern architecture, the parking space was little, the entire mall would be demolished etc etc...but that mall was..." his eyes were widened to look at such a wonderful piece of modern architecture, 'perfectly in its original shape, not even a single piece of brick had been removed.' He thought of something else then suddenly he looked into the newspaper, 'this is the very same newspaper which had written more news against this mall. But now it is printing the ads of this mall, how strange! Is it the case that an illegal mall has turned into a legal one, is it that they have received all the permissions? When and how?'

'Huh..h, why are you so bothered?' After a great effort he could succeed in bringing himself out from the circle of thoughts and questions, he jerked his head; he threw away the newspaper in hand, he opened a pouch Gutka(a kind of mixture eaten with betel leaves) gulped it and entered into a cinema-hall of the same mall to watch a movie.

The name of the movie was 'Blackmail.'

CHAPTER THIRTY-SIX

His Pain

Passengers of the bus were enjoying the news of a cricket match with a neighboring country, they were excited, were waiting for the moment to come, when the results would be in favor of our country. All of them were excitingly speaking in loud voice, some were even shouting slogans, except Rahul who was murmuring, “It would be so good that such matches do not occur.”

“Why? Why should not such matches occur?” Ramprakash, listening to his murmurs asked him very angrily, “Why are you so bothered? What enmity you have with our country?”

“I, an enemy!” Annoyingly Rahul said, “Brother, I am not an enemy, I am a citizen of this country, am a resident of a village near to borders. Whenever the neighboring country attacks, first of all it is us who have to bear the circumstances. The results of such matches may be anything but their cruel army shoots guns for sure. If they win they shoot in happiness and in case they are defeated they shoot in madness or in grief. But what is the ultimate outcome of these shootouts? Some get injured while some face casualty in our village. For a week or so we all have to live in much stress. This is the reason why I spoke such things.

CHAPTER THIRTY-SEVEN

Answer to a Joke

"Uncle" A youth travelling in an over-crowded bus said to an old man, "Be seated."

"Where should I sit my child? Is there any a place?"

"You can very well sit on the ground' the youth was in a mood to make a joke, "At least your legs will be relaxed."

"Kid" the old man grew red with anger, "I have been a mountaineer, my legs are not that weak. And for your kind information, my destination is to reach, not to sit, understood." Hearing his harsh voice the youth seemed to be little embarrassed.

"Answer to one of my question" the old man took the command in his hands, "How did you respond to when you used to feel hungry in your childhood?"

"How a very nonsense question is this, uncle!" So easy, I used to shout 'hungry-hungry' like other kids, what else!"

This is the only difference between you and me. Instead of shouting 'hungry-hungry' I used to shout 'food-food'. From my childhood itself I have had concentration towards the result and not towards means. Did you get me?"

CHAPTER THIRTY-EIGHT

Walkout

A meeting of Hats and shoes was going on. The hats were making fun of the shoes. They were continuously making comments sarcastically they were sarcastic for the shoes- is there any comparison between a hat and a shoe? How can they compare themselves to a crown or a throne...How dare do the shoes to compare themselves with the hats...

When the metaphorical analogies extended unto the extreme level the shoes couldn't stop themselves. They amongst themselves decided and they put forward some of the photographs in front in the meeting. In these photos were some pictures of hats worn by different people of different status, who have had put their heads on their boss's shoes, were cleaning their shoes, some were putting on shoes to their boss. While all these attempts many of the hats have had been fallen down on the shoes of their boss.

Seeing all these things, the hats were a bit nervous resulting into a complete silence. They could not speak up a single word. Feeling embarrassed all the hats walked off from the meeting...

The shoes within their hearts thanked the flattery culture.

CHAPTER THIRTY-NINE

Future's Voice

"The Past said, "What is the Present without me?"

The Present said, "I am the foundation of future, without me there would be no existence of the future."

Looking at them the Future tense said, "I can only say this much that in all times; people have spend and lost money only to know me from amongst all the other tenses.

And in the opposite side of the road, there was a crowd who had gathered for the booking for knowing their future.

CHAPTER FORTY

At the Crossroads of Confusion

'But Madam, that Sir on the fourth number was saying that the weight machine is with you.' The argument was going on in the office, "It is you who will weigh the article and give a ticket."

"Hey ! Just now I had told you that or I had told to someone else?" the lady working on that window said this very angrily, "he will weigh it and I shall give you a ticket, go to him and ask the weight."

"You mean to say that, I who have had wasted so much of time waiting here should now go to him to ask the weight and again come to you and wait and waste one or one and half hour to buy a ticket?" Why is it not possible that both the tasks be fulfilled on a single window? Are you all making a fool of me? Do you think I am worthless person?" His voice was growing high.

"Don't just shout over here and just move aside. We have some more customers, just move aside."

"Today I will have to launch a complaint against this lady, they consider people as fools, I shall make a complaint immediately against you and your rude nature." He shouted more loudly that the people standing around him were in panic and they started staring at him.

Looking at the man going to launch a complaint two of the employees started chatting in loud voice, it was clearly audible to that man, "It seems that Sharma Madam will win today. Madam had already wanted somebody to launch a complaint against her so that she is freed from that window." That person was shocked, "Oh! So this is the case! So the drama is being done for the same reason."He suddenly stopped and he turned back without complaining on the crossroad.

He met one of his old known person namely Akram Bhai, who was a retired person from the same office, he narrated to him the whole incidence to which he said, "And you turned back hearing to what the two of them said? Hey, you would have complained in any case. You are now trapped in their net. This was a conspiracy between Mrs. Sharma and the two flattering people who did not want that anybody should put a complaint against them. You should go and put a complaint." As soon as Akram bhai said this he rode away immediately.

He felt that he was not standing in a city, rather he was standing on a crossroad of confusion wherein he could not judge which road would lead to fight against the chaos.

CHAPTER FORTY-ONE

Fugacious, human being

"Yaar, why is it so that our life span is so short and human beings have a longer life span?" A dog was asking to another dog.

"You are talking of life-span of human beings, right! How come it is larger?" The dog unveiled the suspense while hiding dried roti beneath the sand. "Their life-span is rather very small, very very small. From the day he is born till he is being given a name. That is actually his real life-span. May be; a couple of days or months. After he gets his name then when does he remain as a human-being, actually then he is either a Hindu, a Christian, a Muslim etc.etc.

CHAPTER FORTY-TWO

Knife of Clothes (!)

Somebody was feeling very happy while looking at the colorful flags which were being fixed; someone distributed sweets others were looking at them with great anger.

The only one that trembled was the Earth.

One more partition was sure.

CHAPTER FORTY-THREE

Very Good

He was in off mood after returning from his office. And why shouldn't he be so! For a very small mistake he was scolded by his boss in front of his colleagues and subordinates. His colleagues were staring at him with strange expressions while he was coming out of his office. Was it for sympathy or something else, who knows! He had switched off his phone as it was often ringing which was irritating him, without even attending a single call. While returning, he very unwillingly greeted the people whom he usually met almost daily. For no reason he thought that this Raju Panwala, this Rafeeq Automobile-wala and Dubeyji from his neighbor-hood were looking at him with a waggish look...

While he was just seated on his sofa, after putting off his shoes and socks barbarously and in glumness threw them on a side, his seven years old son Chintoo came and stood in front of him and showed his copy , "Papa, Papa, look at this, teacher has given me, "Very good" at four places.

For a moment he did feel that he should slap his son and tear off his copy, any how he could control over his emotions. He wiped out the sweat, with a very heavy heart and a great effort he could bring a smile on his face, he took his son on his laps and started inspecting his copy, "You Debauch! I shall stop your increment, I will suspend you, will eat away your job" the Boss's harsh words were still echoing into his ears, but while turning its pages some words came out from his mouth, "Very Good, V...e...r...y good, very good!"

CHAPTER FORTY-FOUR

Era of Commodity Market

While he was reading, 'The theory of Supply and demand', just then a milkman came to him to clear-up the previous month's bill. "Hunh! Irritatingly he pushed away the book, table and chair and went out to clear the milkman's bill. Suddenly he recollected that he had already paid Rs. 500/- extra in the previous month and at that time he had said that he would adjust in the next bill amount. He conveyed this to the milkman, but in return the milkman very clearly denied to this, " No bhaiya, you had paid against the milk taken."

He was shocked, after thinking over and talking excessively regardless to this still the milkman did not agree to it then he had paid him seven day's amount of the present month and asked him not to come from the next month.

He was shaken up with this dishonest deed and disgustingly, sitting inside he once again started reading – the thing which is unavailable in the market, which has no stock, its demand increases... "Honesty too is disappearing from within the society" he was once again shaken-up, "then why not its demand and importance is being increased by anyone?"

... "No", saying this he tried to console himself, "No way! Honesty is not a commodity.." and he once again started reading.

CHAPTER FORTY-FIVE

Starving Voice

"Now that it seems that our problem would be solved." Two young ladies, terrified with their over-weight, were discussing on bus-stand, "From this Thursday, Dr. Amit is arriving in our city who is a well-known surgeon, who normalizes the body completely. He has done successful surgery thus decreasing about 10-10, 15-15 kilo of weight."

"What does the doctor thus do in surgery?"

"It seems that he shortens the size of the pouch within the stomach resulting in lessening the feeling of hunger."

"Can't such a pouch be removed from the body?" Listening to them, a man, fully drenched in hunger, a young man suddenly uttered.

CHAPTER FORTY-SIX

Smile of the legs

"Why should I call her?" He was grumbling in himself, " why should I lower down my nose? Let her call me if she so wishes. Why should ...?"

Hearing to so many "Why" both of his legs smiled at looking at the other leg, "When a person wishes to put forward a pace then it is us who stuck up with our own ego.

CHAPTER FORTY-SEVEN

An Empire

On one Friendship-day a dispute between 'management' and 'mismanagement' as to how many friends do each one of them have?

"My friends are," the 'management' could not add a number ahead, "cleanliness, morality, discipline and and...."

"Ha ha ha", with scattered dirty and yellow teeth, the mismanagement exclaimed, "Is that all ! is the list of your friends completed? And who so ever you have mentioned, where are these seen? Now listen to my friends who are spread all over and count- damaged roads, pits, dirty water, mosquitoes, sewage, pigs rolling into filth, depraved and non-working fans, non-working lights, broken and damaged chairs, scattered plaster, banana-peels... how many more should I count? And yes, I completely forgot to mention 3 of my best friends... in-discipline, corruption and laziness."

CHAPTER FORTY-EIGHT

Word and Thing

From among the crowd slogans were being cried out- all of you just look at this, we are all one, Hail with our integrity... "Look here, I am that word" hearing to the most enthusiastic word 'Integrity' proudly said, "the one which considers the crowd together.'

"And I am that thing" currency responded to the word with an intention to break its pride, "I am that remote which when comes on its own then such integrity will collapse within no time, just watch."

Someone from the crowd showered currency notes, everybody in the crowd stopped crying for slogans and now were busy collecting money.

CHAPTER FORTY-NINE

Lord Clive of the Present Century

I was going through newspaper while having food-

Once again a farmer committed suicide, the data statistics of the state farmers has crossed number of fifty.

And some irresponsible statement from responsible person-

"Why do the farmers commit suicide, why don't they pay off compensation by selling their land."

"Farmers should stop farming! Crops can be purchased from foreign lands."

"The cultivated crops may get rotten in warehouses, but shall not be taken out for free distribution"

"to hell with, these old boring news," I threw away the newspaper, lifted up a spoon and started eating some fast food. Chappattis remained untouched in the plate.

The Chinese food which was smiling a few moments earlier was now laughing aloud.

CHAPTER FIFTY

Not only necklace

“Should I make you a gold necklace?” a husband who had received his balance arrears happily asked his wife.

“Surely yes.” Wife said down-heartedly.

“Aren’t you happy?” While looking into his wife’s eyes he asked.

“Yes I am! But look at this.” Showing news of chain-snatching in the newspaper she said giving a sigh, “Nineteenth century wives may have felt happy after receiving golden chains from their husband but presently if you want to purchase me a necklace then better purchase me a mobile first so that incase if the necklace gets robbed than the police can be called immediately.

CHAPTER FIFTY-ONE

Speech of Fungus

Bottles of glucose were being packed in a factory. Two fungus webs hanging on the ceiling were discussing, "Yesterday there was a call from Yamdoot (a messenger of the god of death) he was thanking us. He was saying that it is because of you, your bottles containing glucose had us as its content it was possible to have completed my target. Else one increment of mine would have been stopped.

"In this what is our role?" The other web laughed, "The modern kalyug people should be thanked for whose carelessness it is possible that we are locked into glucose bottles and the users fell severely ill, thus lose lives."

"Yes, you are right else how our names would come in newspapers and television.

CHAPTER FIFTY-TWO

Slap

On one early morning of Environment Day, a famous social institution organized a cycle rally, but at the last moment it was changed into walker's rally.

The reason, majority of the members of the institution had four-four, six-six petrol automobiles, but had no cycle.

CHAPTER FIFTY-THREE

Security Not Needed

Ramakant was fed up of the rats in the house. In every room, every corner, they would blow great guns for all twenty four hours. Rats! Of all sizes from small to as large as a cat. But for religion fearing he did not want to kill them, only wanted to drive them off. One day he brought a cat from somewhere, having bigger and scary eyes. He started taking care and feeding her. All went well for two days, it seemed that the rats had been driven off, but then it was the same. The rats had become bolder and without any fear they would eat, scatter and destroy grains, clothes, books, bed and even plastic items. On the other side the cat would eagerly wait for milk and cream. She did not even bother to look at the rats. Now he had to worry about milk and ghee. Ramakant was extremely unhappy that he could not make a way out of this problem.

But then he did not have to ponder for long. One noon while he was resting on his bed, he saw a rat taking out a piece of sweet from a rack and keeping it in front of the cat. The cat didn't even pay attention towards the rat, rather she pounced over on sweets.

Ramakant understood the mystery behind the rats being so fearless, for which he immediately decided to drive off the cat from his house.

CHAPTER FIFTY-FOUR

Aren't we girls!

Twelve years old Nikita and ten years old Amita were alone at home. Their five years old the only brother, had gone to attend a marriage ceremony with their parents. The two sisters were looking at the photos in an old album.

"Look at this didi, the first photo of our brother after he was just born, this is his first birthday photo. We two are standing behind."

"Yes, and look at this, his first photo of his first footsteps he had taken, so many of them. How much sweet is our brother isn't he?"

"But didi, there are so many photos of our brother in these albums, but only two-three photos of ours. Why so?" Seeing at one sided relationship the young Amita could not stop herself asking such a question.

"We are girls after all!" The elder one gave an explanation.

CHAPTER FIFTY-FIVE

Commercial Vision

After twenty three years they were returning to their hometown. They were eager to know about their birthplace, childhood days and were thinking out it. Their heartbeat was running fast as their train was arriving nearer to the city. They would peep out from the window and were trying to recollect their childhood memories, which were buried in their lost memories, but they were struggling hard to bring them out- Desainagar crossed, this is Bahadur ganj, this might be Saryu chawl, all has drastically changed. "Hey?" just then they were shaken as if they had recollected something and they all of sudden uttered, "Where have the hills which were outside the city disappeared where there were so many deep trees? We would climb up on the hill-top right? Previously those hills could be clearly visible from the running trains.

"Uncle", hearing to their talks a traveler said, "Your hills have been removed, now those hills have been transferred into colonies, this is the reason that you could not know."

"Is it?" they were once again shocked, "such wonderful hills have been cut down? Houses have developed? Those hills were a great grandeur for the city, in our times."

"During your time the world would measure the hills in square-feet's and when was anything of such thing ever occur?"

CHAPTER FIFTY-SIX

A Deep Well of Negativity

As soon as Rammohanji secured passed out in B.E. securing good marks, within no time he got a job in a nearby big factory. 'Something is better than nothing' with this thought he on the very first day went into officer's chamber, "Come in" Assistant manager half-heartedly said, "What job should I give you? Do one thing, go and bring four-five labors, a motor-pump has fallen down into the well near the main gate, try to remove it. Today do this, later on we shall decide."

Rammohanji was in tediousness, a B.E. holder and to remove a motor from a well! Yet, he brought five labors and reached near the well and made an inspection. The well was very big and deep, with lot of water in it. It was a great risk removing the motor from out of the well. Still, considering it as a duty with his labors he engrossed himself in the task.

After hours of hard-work by evening the motor-pump could be removed and was kept on the wall of the well. He felt contended after succeeding his first task in his first job. The officials rushed to that place after getting the news, "Has the motor-pump been taken out? How had it fallen into the well?"

Rammohanji was astonished, "How did it fall? No applaud, nor any word of appreciation! How did it fell? Very promptly did he pushed the motor pump from the wall into the well and shouted, "This is how it had fallen! How much efforts, daring and risks had I taken to remove it. None of you made an attempt to ask how did I remove it?"

Rammohanji was removed from his job with a charge of indiscipline. While he was returning he was thinking as to when we would succeed in from coming out from a deep well of negativity and ask how it was removed.

Printed by Libri Plureos GmbH in Hamburg,
Germany